ANCHOR BOOKS

PURPLE HAZE

Edited by

Sarah Marshall

First published in Great Britain in 2003 by
ANCHOR BOOKS
Remus House,
Coltsfoot Drive,
Peterborough, PE2 9JX
Telephone (01733) 898102

HB ISBN 1 84418 180 4
SB ISBN 1 84418 181 2

FOREWORD

Anchor Books is a small press, established in 1992, with the aim of promoting readable poetry to as wide an audience as possible.

We hope to establish an outlet for writers of poetry who may have struggled to see their work in print.

The poems presented here have been selected from many entries, and as always editing proved to be a difficult task.

I trust this selection will delight and please the authors and all those who enjoy reading poetry.

Sarah Marshall
Editor

CONTENTS

THE SNOW

It was a cold, crisp morning, the month was January,
The temperature outside was as chilly as could be.
I looked up in the sky, there were no clouds at all
And then suddenly to my amazement, I saw some snowflakes fall.
The snowflakes started to come down thick and fast, turning
                                    everything all white,
To see that snow all falling down was such a beautiful sight.
It kept snowing more and more, covering all the roofs and trees,
It was falling soft and gently drifting in the breeze.
People and children were playing in the snow,
Throwing snowballs that they made at each other, to and fro,
Having so much fun with the snowballs in their hand,
Enjoying the special moments of a winter wonderland.
Snow doesn't come that often, it is a truly wonderful sight,
It makes everything outside all beautiful and bright.
Although the snow is cold, the opposite of hot,
It brings joy to a lot of people, leaving them with happy memories
                                    not easily forgot.
So, one last thing to remember is that if you see the snow,
Remember all the fun you can have throwing snowballs to and fro.

Toni Attew

DRAGON LORD!

Majestically he stands - towering over his master,
dwarfing him with his mammoth proportions.
As his outspread wings in purple haze aglow,
awaiting instruction, or to avoid disaster,
so thereby bequeath his lord a show.

It's from within his mist-filled, enormous cavern,
a quagmire of hazardous defences quiver,
enshrouding his existence from the outer world.
Allowing rest and regeneration,
till once again he ventures to come forth.

A single beam of light penetrates the dark,
from the gaping orifice up high - stark.
The entrance of his personal domain,
where he shelters for his periodical refrain.

Stalagmite and stalactites abound,
decorating his lair from ceiling to ground.
While insignificant, slithery creatures unseen
are so unpretentiously strewed,
flying and scurrying at every sound.

Disenfranchised from those of his own kind,
still he struggles and serves a mystic mind.
Until some day control is lost,
releasing him finally with horrendous cost,
becoming his own master and boss.

Gary J Finlay

A BLEAK WINTER'S DAY

I'm old, gone grey, with many white hairs,
The terrible truth is - nobody cares.
I'm sad, I'm lonely, forgotten and grey
With no one to talk to day after day.
I look from my window hoping to see
A glimpse of a person, other than me.
Not a single soul, no one comes past,
They jump in their cars and go very fast.
I have plenty to do - books to read
Television to watch, I can fill every need.
I keep snug and warm from the weather outside,
I count my blessings, to be cheerful - I've tried.
I'm old and I'm lonely, because you see
There's no one to talk to - other than me.
There's a knock at the door! They're not going past!
I can hardly believe it - a visitor at last.

Shirley Joy Dean

A DISAPPOINTING SPRING

'Spring is in the air,' said the jeweller,
As he eased the back off my watch.
He assured me that he was a qualified man
And that he was not there to botch.
He admitted he was trained on digitals
And was not a chronological man,
But he'd have a crack at my prized time-piece,
Because you've got to get work where you can.
I rue the day I met him,
It was an absolute drag.
I still have my valuable time-piece,
It's all at home, in pieces, in a paper bag.

Trevor Napper

THE LONGEST DAY

What do they mean by the longest day?
There must be more time to go out and play,
So why should I be called in from play,
When the sky is as bright as day.

No night-time has reached the sky.
So why, oh why
Am I told it's time for bed
After all, it is the longest day, so they said.

Katherine Parker

THE SUMMER FETE

Roll up! Roll up! For the school summer fete,
Come along in, it'll be just great!
The sun is out, the sky is blue,
There's plenty of marvellous things to do.

Games and stalls, books and toys,
Voices, laughter, lots of noise.
Hot dogs, cold drinks in the dining hall,
Pay at the gate, there's something for all.

A police car and an ice cream van,
Ice creams being sold by a fireman!
The fire engine's come as well,
Flashing its lights and ringing its bell.

Here comes the parade for the fancy dress,
Most costumes are good - but that one's a mess.
Parents wave and cameras click -
One little girl has just been sick!

The country dancers are coming out,
Smiling, waving and jumping about.
The music starts and off they go,
Whirling, clapping, their faces aglow.

The raffle's been drawn, prizes announced,
That boy's won a football, watch it bounce!
The money's counted, the stalls put away,
Till the next school fete on another day.

Sue Smith

SUMMERTIME BLUES

Hooray, it's summertime at last.
We hope the sun, as in the past,
Will show its face and give heat,
Some sunbathing for a treat.

But we know what we will get.
Gales and thunder, always wet.
Umbrellas poking, oozing mud,
Frost to kill the opening bud.

No cricket, rain stopped play,
Put off for another day.
Wimbledon, the tennis stopped,
We should have known, summer's flopped.

Then the autumn round again,
Yes, I know, much more rain.
Darker nights, mornings too,
What on earth are we to do?

With melting ice and rising seas,
The country's flooded, if you please.
And with all that water's motion,
We'll soon float off into the ocean.

We would jump for joy and hum
If we moved towards the sun
And if we floated nearer Spain,
We could enjoy our life again.

Harry Gill

HARVEST

First there comes the winter snow,
Then the rough March winds a-blow;
Next, warm sunshine's golden glow,
Ripening nut and berry.

Cornfields ripple in the breeze,
Fruits hang heavy on the trees,
Fish abound in rolling seas,
Gleaned from rock and skerry.

In each church let people praise
For the plenteous harvest days,
Yielding barley, wheat and maize,
Glowing peach and cherry.

Golden honey from the hive,
Juice of grape and humble chive,
Hedgerow berries grow and thrive -
Praise Him and be merry!

F M Reed

SUN SHOWER

See the light that sparkles reflected through the rain,
That pitter-patters down the leaves then drips right off again,
Descending just like diamonds from off a golden crown,
A myriad angels' tears, like pearl drops falling down.

It glistens off the flower heads like tiny crystal balls
And all the world is silent, except for rain that falls.
These fragile little raindrops on cobwebs can be seen,
A miracle of nature, with star drops for a screen.

And as the rain keeps falling, the flowers droop their heads,
In silent contemplation on fertile flower beds.
When soon with ease those minute seeds will wake from sleep
and slumber
By turning into wondrous flowers, too numerous to number.

Through driving rain the birds refrain from flying and they rest
Amongst the ivy on the wall, deep down inside their nest.
From tiny little insects to the biggest ones around,
All seek a place of sweet repose instead of getting drowned.

As soon as it had started, the rain clouds passed away,
Replaced by rays of golden sun reflecting on the day.
When rain-like shafts of arrows fast dropped upon the ground,
Dried up like blotting paper, then let the world resound

To sounds of tiny insects and creatures big and small,
Just working at their daily tasks as though it never rained at all.
Right back to where they started, as busy as can be,
And make the best of sunny days, whenever they may be.

It doesn't rain all the time in your life,
So when it stops . . . you start.

Robert Eric Weedall

THANK YOU

I was born in May at the end of spring,
Waiting for summer its jewels to bring
And little I knew as the days passed by
That year after year with swift-changing sky
Would provide me with beauties freshly to sing.

Daisies were first, gold heart and white frill;
Buttercup riches, gorse on the hill,
Roses in gardens, spilling their scent,
Butterflies dancing wherever one went,
Sunflowers with honey-bees drinking their fill.

Next, apples and plums on bent autumn trees,
Leaves that changed colour to fly on the breeze,
Blue morning mists and cobwebs like gauze,
Harvest-time's revels before winter's pause -
Fortunate children with treasures like these!

Year follows year with winter's delights;
Robin's song, carols and long cosy nights,
Christmas to welcome with bells pealing clear,
Tightly-packed stockings - what shall we find here?
Then New Year to lead us to springtime's sights.

Many years pass, but their joys still remain -
Snowdrops and primroses, soft April rain -
Ninety years onward I see them with love
And gladly give thanks to the Father above
Who orders the earth like a joyous refrain,
Its climax at Easter, again and again.

Kathleen M Hatton

A RELAXED DAY

The sun was really shining,
Warming up my pool.
Sipping iced tea, I was,
Before soaking up the sun.
It was nearly lunchtime,
So sandwiches I had,
Then with only just my trunks on,
Relaxed and soaked up the sun.
If I got hot,
I'd dive and so be cool.

M D Bedford

GLORIOUS AUTUMN

Beautiful sunlight filtering through the trees,
Dappling the ground covered in leaves
Autumn has arrived in all its splendour
September, October and November.

Foggy, damp mornings when fungi appear
Bracken, fern dying
Exposing the deer.

The days growing shorter, sun not as strong
Unlike the spring, hardly any birds' song.
Squirrels collecting their winter store
Of nuts from the trees and the woodland floor.

Berries and abundance
Fill the hedgerows.
Autumn in all its glory,
When the countryside glows.

Christine Hardemon

ONLY A WINTER'S SONNET

Winter is the time of year I don't like the best,
It's miserable and soggy and it's cold,
I know that summertime is unpredictable at best,
But sometimes then at least the sun shines gold.
Some folks like nothing better than to go out in the snow
And freeze their wotsits off and call it fun,
But I like spring and summer best, cos skiing I don't go,
And winter is a right pain in the bum!
I know it looks all decorative on Christmas cards and such
And gathering round the fire is very nice,
But when all's said and done, I don't like winter very much.
I'm not a fan of storms and snow and ice;
I s'pose to sum it up, winter is my idea of Hell,
So someone else can have my share as well!

Mick Nash

THE SEASONS

When buds burst forth and blossoms bloom
And the honeysuckle draws the bee
And a sweet fragrance is in the air
And you feel as content as can be,
Will your thoughts run to me?

When you stroll down by the river
And sit under a shady tree
And the green summer leaves they shimmer
And the sweet songbird you see,
Will your thoughts run to me?

When the leaves they change colour
And wither and blow away
And the branches on the trees lie bare
And you recall another day,
Will your thoughts run to me?

When the robin is tucked up in his nest
And you feel the frosty air
And you remember the dreams of yesterday,
The ones that we did share,
Will your thoughts run to me?

Joan Magennis

SEASONS

Winter, summer, autumn and spring
Those are the four seasons,
Different feelings they all bring
And all with special reasons.

Winter brings the snow
And winds that make you cold,
Yet it makes your heart glow
With a feeling that can't be told.

Summer brings the sun
To brighten all the day,
With picnics and all that fun,
Plus love for every day.

Autumn makes the leaves fall,
Dropping one by one,
With happiness and joy for all,
It is a special one.

Spring brings the leaves back,
Fighting autumn's will,
Helping us to get back
A joy, our hearts to fill.

All these seasons together
Make one year complete.
Come again next year,
The story we shall repeat.

Funmilayo Ojedokun (12)

SUMMER SUNSET

Amber glow and azure hue,
This sky, burnished, once was blue;
Gold globe of sun has vanished now
That eventide begins its show.

Green, leafy summer is the stage
As August turns another page,
Screaming gulls fly overhead -
Silver feathers glisten red.

With this sunset's vivid streak,
Waiting for the spell to break;
Dusk's curtain deepens, shadows shade
Within the dimness of this glade.

As one day dies, another's born -
Soon comes the whisper of the dawn.

Lyn Dickson

THOUGHTS AT THE TURNING OF THE YEAR

In the depths of winter I yearn for spring,
For the seasons, like fragile flowers,
Are such transient things.
This midwinter may be bleak or savage,
Ravaged by blinding, ice-scouring rain,
The white-out of some great blizzard,
Or frost-bound ground as hard as nails.
Last autumn saw the importance
Of planting a bounty of spring flowers.
Set a display, a superlative bouquet
For the fey months of March to May,
Though spring lay many months way.
Planted prim primrose and gay polyanthus,
Sky blue forget-me-nots and gillyflowers.
The well-bred descendents of the wild daisies
All jostling for prime position,
Vying, as glamorous garden neighbours,
Along with corms and bulbs of every sort.
Snowdrops, grape hyacinths and crocus
And drifts of golden daffodils, of course.
Then I really went to town
With the rainbow of tulips I found.
So too, many hyacinths went into pots,
An end of season special offer,
A local shop sold off as job lots.
And do you know what?
I've just found the first flowering snowdrop.
As I stand at the door of the new year,
For the passing year, I shed not a tear.

Jonathan Pegg

FROST PAINTS WHITE

Frost lays white the early morn,
The eastern sun burns cold at dawn.
The brave birds still herald light,
Tucked singing within foliage tinged white.
Frozen water sparkles ice-clear,
While the rosy glow in a steely sky brings cheer.
Frosty crystals glisten a February day,
Decorating with diamond jewels, the bleak made gay.
Silver hoar on the hedgerows is in shimmering array,
As this frost paints white, bright over winter grey.

Carol Ann Darling

MIDWINTER

A deep depression over England
Marching out to meet the earth
Rich and fertile, muddy fields
Tractors bringing sugar beet
From whence they'll go to Bury town.

Not a soul I met on country walks
Suffolk lost - so melancholy
Puddles lay in country lanes
Dripping branches - windswept trees
Ditches full and waterlogged.

A vicarage light through the gloom
In summertime, its gardens green
Open to the public - Red Cross teas
Now silent, full of dead chrysanthemums
Remnants of a season past.

All is still with hedgerows bare
December so disconsolate
But there is hope at Christmastide
A ray of sunshine - Christian warmth
Life goes on in Stowlangtoft.

Steve Glason

RAVISHING SPRING

Snowdrops in their white array
Daffodils make a beautiful spray
Hyacinths in their coats of blue
Primulas in radiant hue
Bluebells chiming in field and forest
Primroses always look at their best
Lilies with their trumpets wide and white
What a beautiful, heavenly sight
Ravishing spring uplifts all our dreary hearts
And joyfully ends our wintry aching parts.

Alma Montgomery Frank

SPRINGTIME

Today I saw a little squirrel
Scamper through the trees.
The nights are lighter;
Mornings warmer,
Daffodils, tulips, bluebells bright,
All frolic in the breeze.
Cherry blossom peeps at me -
And the almond looks divine.
Everything is waking up,
Another spring is here.
The birds are singing in delight,
Their nests they start to build.
New life, new life is what I see,
Another spring is here.

Janet Cavill

SPRING IN CORNWALL

The rich earth thrives with life,
The sun tips every shimmering bough,
Birds are singing with the dawn,
They know it's spring somehow.
Flowers unfurl to show their heads,
Their colours all ablaze,
Caught like a delicate butterfly wing
In the misty morning haze.
The woods show coloured carpets
Of blue and gold and green,
Their beauty fresh, uncovered,
Are the prettiest ever seen.
Waves crash onto rugged rocks
Then hit the golden sand,
The pale spring sunshine filters through
To warm the barren land.
The skyline filled with screaming gulls,
Who squabble, fight and dive
For fish that may be carried
On the waves that seem alive.
Every corner picturesque,
The woods, the land, the sea,
Nature's beauty dwells right here
And will always be part of me,
It's where I wish to end my days
As it's in my heart, from birth,
And it's where my soul will be content
When I'm laid in its rich brown earth.

This is my Cornwall in the spring,
A natural, wondrous land,
Set in the heart of the country
And painted by nature's hand,
Overflowing with beauty for everyone to see,
The only place to live and die,
The only heaven for me . . .

Margaret Hanning

SPRING HAS SPRUNG

I've noticed little crocuses
Growing in my pot.
They've opened purple petals out
For all the world to spot.

I've seen the yellow daffodils
Sway gently in the breeze.
They're dancing slowly to and fro
Right underneath the trees.

I've watched the fluffy newborn lambs
All running in the sun.
They're skipping round and round the fields,
It really looks like fun.

I've realised that spring is here,
It quite crept up on me.
There's Easter eggs and hot-cross buns,
I'm happy as can be!

Kaz

THE TEMPTRESS

Spring is like a temptress
Who lures you to her arms
With her warm embraces
And exquisite charms.

She beckons you to walk with her
And sit by waters blue
And marvel at her beauty
Adorned with nature's dew.

Do not trust her lovely face
Nor promises to thrill
When darkness hides her beauty
She breathes an icy chill.

Helen T Westley

PROMISE

You bold, black branches against the winter sky,
Tell us, so weary of winter, if the spring is nigh?
You keep your leafy secrets till the sun is high -
Tell us, so weary of winter, can the spring be nigh?

See my bold, black branches, comes the tree's reply,
And the tracery of twigs against the winter sky?
Each bears its tiny buds till spring is nigh,
Keeping its leafy secrets till the sun is high.

But when the snowdrops wither and the lark sings high,
The daffodils will trumpet that the spring is nigh,
Then my leaves will dance a greeting to each bird and butterfly
A welcome! To spring's hope and beauty, and to winter's
                                        cold - goodbye!

Mary Dimond

SPRINGTIME

Spring a lovely sight to see, flowers struggling to be free
Pansies arrive in all their colours; grace the garden to be sure
All these flowers year after year, give us hope I do declare
Snow from winter is now gone, spring is gently coming on

When we see the daffodils, know that spring is coming fast
Bluebells also amid the grass, tinkle too as we walk past
Tiny snowdrops lift their heads; see the crocus in their beds
Some are yellow, some are blue, even white and purple too

More daylight as summer comes, grass is growing, time to mow
Busy bees making honey, they work hard when it's sunny
Time to plant the garden beds, maybe paint the garden shed
Chat to neighbours at the fence, lovely flowers, lovely scent

Now to plant the trees and roses, garden rubbish for disposal
Don't work too hard, have some time for sport and games
Take a holiday, cruise maybe, lots of sights for you to see
See the lovely Scottish heather, best to view in sunny weather

Spring, like youth feels so good, so much promise in every bud
The sun, and flowers feel the touch; life is on the up and up
Even when the spring has gone, know that summer follows on
Like the world is born free, spring's arrived for you and me.

Joan Prentice

SPRING

Spring is here
Let out a cheer
Dark days are done
Welcome the sun

Snowdrops are in bloom
Daffodils will be soon
The crocuses display
In the lengthening day

On hedgerow and bough
Buds are bursting now
And in grass and wood
Bluebells are coming good

Spring is all around us
And nature is in such a fuss
Which is the very reason
For such a lovely season.

Derek Spencer

SPRINGTIME

Spring comes dancing down the way
Winter is now left far behind,
Now snowdrops and the crocus bloom
A sight that gladdens every mind.

Male blackbirds now sing their song
Fuelled by a testosterone rise,
Whilst young men's thoughts turn to love
Accompanied with aching sighs.

The hedgehogs from their sleep do wake
And on a night go out to feed,
On anything their fancy takes
For they need strength for them to breed.

The catkins on the willow trees
Give us a most delightful show
And daffodils sway in the breeze
Their trumpets give a golden glow.

Come spring the ramblers walk the hills
Aided by firm, stout walking sticks,
Whilst in the valleys farmers take
Deliveries of day-old chicks.

The season of nature's reproduction,
When birds and beasts bond into pairs
And we stand by in sheer amazement
To watch a boxing match of hares.

Frantically gardeners till the soil,
A-making beds to sow the seeds,
The problem is that nature's faster
In germinating seeds of weeds.

Spring, nature's time for recreation
Ah me, I'm past my prime for copulation.

David A Garside

HOPEFUL SPRING?

Spring is in the air once more
Opening the heart to hope again,
Uplifting us to the very core,
Freeing us from darkness and pain.

But what will it hold for you and me
With the overpowering threat of war?
How can we allow ourselves to be
Filled with hope and joy once more?

Colour returns to the garden and fills
Our minds with excitement and fun,
An end to grey days and sudden chills,
With an open invitation to the sun.

But times are threatening and dire,
Faced, as we are, by unknown fears
Of destruction by bombs or fire,
A future beset by horror and tears.

Let us hope spring's magic will
Work miracles and we can dream
It will spread its vibrant message until
All is resolved and peace reigns supreme!

S J Dodwell

SPRING IN THE AIR

Snowdrops, daffodils, crocus abound
Life anew coming up from the ground
New shoots on trees, dew on the grass
These are a few of nature's ways come to pass
Frolicking lambs, young calves and ponies
Spring in the air for the birds and the drone bees
Nature waking up, filled with new zest
Birds in the air, to the young in their nest
Piglets, chicks, new life on the farm
Just some of life's beauty, biologic charm
It doesn't end there, life's beauties abound
Open your eyes, take a look around
Young fish in the rivers, the sea or stream
This is our world, it is no dream
Spring comes every year, right on the dot
Forever and a day whether you like it or not
New birth, renewal, the beginning, restart
Each year we have spring, till death do us part
Don't moan at the rain or the ice on the earth
The sun will soon shine at our world's rebirth
For all this is our inheritance, do not despair
A new world is born, spring is in the air.

Carl Fricker

ZEBEDEE

Here we are now entering spring
Throughout winter in the garden we've done nothing.
It is time to attend to the soil,
So for a few days at this we toil
Breaking up all the lumps,
Throwing dead stuff on our rubbish dumps,
Getting rid of the numerous weeds,
Putting in new plants and seeds.
We will soon see our efforts gain
After a light shower of warm rain.
Buds and leaf now starting to show through
And the sky is turning lighter blue.
It will not be long
Before birds start again with song,
After this they will build a nest,
For a time they don't get much rest.
Easter arrives and we are given an egg,
It gets warmer and women show more leg.

S Glover

SPRING

Now, at winter's close, hasten the spring
And the symphony of colour the season's birth will bring,
When bulb and corm and tuber dormant for nigh a year
Respond to Nature's call as she bids their growth
And the winter hidden flora will use the fresh born power
To cover o'er the barren soil with foliage and flower,
The longer days and warmer nights will continue again the scene
And naked trees, waiting stark and bare, are newly clothed in green.
But leaf and twig and branch will, in their turn be overlain
As tree-borne flower and blossom fill the landscape once again.
In nest, in stream, in meadow, above ground and below
Spring's own aphrodisiac will bring new life on show.
Appearing in its time and place overall and countrywide
And this vernal abundance will not be denied,
As this isle becomes a garden, by man and nature laid
And 'twixt sea and channel waters is so wondrously displayed.
The season is also a message of yet warmer days ahead
When summer blooms awake and rise, as spring's are put to bed.
And as Sol's spring rays caress my pallid face
So will my body stir in longing for the summer sun's embrace.

Thomas R Slater

UNDER THE RAINBOW

Gentle April showers, fluffy clouds blown helter-skelter
Oh there's a rainbow under which I shall shelter.
Pot of gold, rainbow's end, legendary treasure trove,
Yet I shall dream, search for riches other, those of love
Health, happiness, kindness, dear precious lot,
True friendship to mention in that celestial pot
'Neath nature's wondrous, colourful umbrella comes to mind
Wealth more desirous than gold in the crock to find
Shimmering sun, soft caressing showers,
April's glory, sweet blossoming flowers,
True beauty one can feel, one can see,
Heavenly, artistic rainbow's arc, blessing you, blessing me.

Christina Craig Harkness

SIMPLY THE BEST

Oh pretty little daffodil in your
Frilly yellow dress, why do you strive
So endlessly to compete with all the rest?
The rose in all her glory with her
Many guises and colours, we choose at
Very special times to give family, friends and lovers.
The tall and slender lily with her
Dainty, drooping head, brings happiness
And sadness and sometimes tears are shed.
So pretty little daffodil in your frilly,
Fluted dress, when springtime comes around
Once more, you simply are the best.

Elizabeth Woonton

WARM MEMORIES OF A CHILDHOOD SPRINGTIME

Uncontrolled excitement flared when spring's sun struggled through,
It meant the clothes of winter cast aside for something new.
Each spring there'd be another coat, the old one now won't do,
Last year it was a green one, so this year's would be blue.

Those colours never varied, it really must be said,
Though they were very pretty, this child longed for a red.
Thoughts of crimson clothing never reached her Mother's head,
Too many other things were there - like getting children fed.

There had to be a hat of straw arrayed in tiny flowers,
Could not wait to put it on a-trembling through s-l-o-w hours.
Nights seemed so long . . . sleep would not come . . . tho' calling
                                                        up all powers
Like counting sheep that ambled past, straight into cooler bowers.

Gloves and coat were donned at last for Sunday morning singtime,
Socks gleaming white with garters tight embedding round leg ringtime.
Elastic battening down straw hat, ensuring painful chintime,
But all was well, the sun was out, and ouch! Another springtime!

Jean B Cardwell

THE RHYTHM OF SPRING

The rhythm of spring vibrates through the earth,
A new season is here, a time for rebirth.
With one sweep, Mother Nature turns greys to green,
Wiping away the dull winter scene.
Once more Nature her timeless role will fulfil,
Bringing forth crocus, snowdrops and daffodil.
The sap rises high bringing life to the tree
Growing buds swelling, bursting to be free.
Small animals from their lairs do creep,
Eyes still heavy from long winter's sleep.
Birds will mate and their song will trill,
The early morning air their music will fill.
Spring lifts the veil of winter's gloom,
Once more to bring love and life into bloom.

Iris Taylor

LET'S SPRING AHEAD!

Hooray, hoorah! Spring has sprung, winter has gone away,
I really enjoy this time of the year, the lengthening of the day.
And as nature's creatures wake themselves, they shake their
sleepy heads,
They adventure out into a brand new world, they leave their
unmade beds.

And so me, a horticulturalist, another dawn, a new beginning,
I prune, I chop, I clip, I split, I give the shrubs a trimming.
The hues and shades of glorification - they've had their day,
they've finished,
Rosettes and clusters of multicolour - they've passed away,
all vanished.

The spits and clods of dark, damp soil, I slowly lift and turn,
The birth of a new gardening year, I wonder what I'll learn?
Nature has an intriguing habit, it conjures up a brand new story,
God's authors all prepare their scripts, they are ready to bask in
all its glory.

Galanthus standing proud and sure, their angelic heads nod and
sway in rhythm,
Narcissus, crocus, aconite bulbs from under the cold dank ground
they've striven,
To begin the ritual of a new gardening year, they are the
prime contenders,
The first to decorate the earth with their many colours of
many splendours.

I pause - I'm working up a sweat from my endeavour and my toil,
I stand transfixed, watch a feathered friend who is searching
through the soil.
He prods and digs, with hooked yellow beak, I stare as it starts
to squirm,
For suddenly he tugs it out, a writhing, fat, juicy worm.

I double dig another trench, I sense anticipation,
I'll soon remove the weeds, the brash, last year's degradation,
Across the garden, my feathered friend is chirping in a tree,
He's trying to drive me onwards - says, 'Whatever will be, will be.

For you and I have struggled, yes! We've made it through the
winter cold,
A brand new year, a new beginning - let's start afresh and leave the old.
You tend your garden, I'll tend my nest, to ignore them would be
a crime,
In ninety days spring will be over and then yes, guess what,
it's summertime.'

Simeon N Walker

SPRINGTIME

Springtime has come at last,
With a warm caress soft winds return,
Beauty follows the smiling sun,
The redbreast sits in the holly bush,
Fresh green appears as leaf buds burst.

Under a sky of cloudless blue,
The pine displays fringes of contrastive hue,
Daffodils stand tall amongst the grass,
Breaking into a golden splash.

Nature shakes her kaleidoscope,
A painted lady flutters about,
Wakened from her butterfly sleep.
On speckled blue eggs sits a thrush,
Firmly staying at her post.

Winter has fled, snow melts fast,
The hidden stream chuckles and laughs.
Wild flowers spread a colourful cloth,
The cuckoo calls, a solitary bird,
His simple notes stir the soul, touch the heart.

The wooded slopes are bluebell-clad,
Green leaves glisten with drops of dew.
High in the blue sings the lark,
Springtime has come at last.

Beth Izatt Anderson

I WATCHED

I watched the leaves swirl gently
As they fluttered to the ground
Graceful as a ballerina
As they swayed to autumn's sounds.

I watched the leaves swirl gently
From the branch of the old oak tree
They danced across the frosty grass,
Stopping to acknowledge me!

I watched the leaves swirl gently
As they danced up to the gate,
What is that sound,
Are they singing? *It's late, it's late, it's late!*

I watched the leaves swirl gently
As they played in the autumnal mist
The wind whipped up its golden treasures
With the lightest touch, my cheek it kissed.

I watched the leaves swirl gently
As they wait for winter's song.
Autumn, oh how I embrace your beauty,
I've waited for you the seasons long.

Sylvia Connor

Spring Is In The Air

Who told the tiny violets to open up and softly glow,
The tall, imperious daffodils, their trumpets now to blow?
Who dressed the plum in its bridal gown of blossom pure as snow,
To liberally scatter confetti with each wayward breezy blow?
The sweetly dreaming bluebell is awakened by the tune,
Does the same voice whisper, 'No, not yet, but very, very soon.'?
The birds have heard their wake-up call they answer with a will,
So much to do, so little time, with nests to build and fill.
Ambling badgers patrol again, whilst all is dark and still,
Random frosts do not deter, despite the bitter chill.
If we but listen we could hear spring's message loud and clear,
The whisper comes from one above, a vow renewed each year
That springtime follows winter's ills, as night will follow day,
Give heartfelt thanks to Him above for every lovely day.

G Halliwell

MAGNOLIA TREE

Oh, come to see my Magnolia tree
On this beautiful spring day
Come into the garden room
And view its grand display

Sit down into an easy chair
Take a footstool, take your ease
With cup in hand now rest awhile
Linger here until you please

Take in its glorious splendour
Of petals pink and creamy white
In the gentle breeze they dance and sway
In the yellow, warm sunlight

Oh, come and see my Magnolia tree
Pass not such beauty by
For winter's darkness ebbs away
And long summer days are nigh.

Trish Duxbury

THE SPIRIT OF OUR WOODLAND

Summoning colleagues in vast numbers
The Greenman stirs from winter's slumbers.
Releasing spring to a budding start,
Chlorophyll surges through woodland's heart.
On Nature's pallet, greens are blended
Their many shades in leaves suspended,
Branches clothed in glorious green,
The vestments of spring are truly seen.

These evolving wonders each displayed
As shapes and colours all parade,
Sheltered by trees, purple violets grow,
Yellow primroses with celandines show.
In a silver stream, brown water voles
Beneath sage willows, kingfishers' holes.
Red squirrels barely touch the ground
From dreys where coned pines abound.

We would lack Nature's varied plan
Without our generous Greenman.
Carpets of bluebells would have no shade,
Or green woodpeckers a woodland glade.
Arboreal splendours could suffer
If conservation is not tougher.
Those avenues the Greenman sustains
Should be saved from destructive claims.

H D Hensman

THE FIRST BREATH OF SPRING

The March winds give a gentle tease
As one walks in the bracing breeze.
Flowers shoot up everywhere,
Pale green buds appear
Upon the landscape far and near.

Children dance about with delight
As they can now fly their kite.
The world awakes from its winter sleep,
Baby birds emerge to take a peep
At the new world about them.

Newborn lambs frolic in the sun,
From their lair, fox cubs come out to play.
In the woods, comes the call of the cuckoo,
Greeting the spring with, 'How do you do?'
The blossom spreads so white and fair,
The first breath of spring is in the air.

B C Rice

CELTIC SPRING

Fresh breezes blow - skies cloudless blue;
Smile and all nature smiles with you.
Streams flow with crystal currents all,
Fed by the sparkling waterfall.
The horse herd gathers on the brink,
Dilating nostrils ere they drink,
While in the meadow new green-clad
Contented cattle munch full glad.

The fields wear garlands down and up,
Daisy and cowslip, buttercup;
In bush and coppice blackbirds sing
And April cuckoo heralds spring.
Now in the wood the fresh-leaved beech
Allows the eager sun to reach
And rustling branches in the tree
Play soft their own sweet symphony.

Gwym measures out the plough-land length
Rejoicing in his manhood's strength;
Fresh from her milking, with soft dew
Gwen will her blushing cheeks renew.
This happy, holy, springtime hour
Goodwill bursts forth, a brighter flower –
Nature's in love these fair spring days
And sings her kind Creator's praise.

Barrie Williams

SPRING SONG

There's something in the air,
A whisper everywhere,
A fluttering of birds on the wing
And the world is alive with joyful song -
It is spring.

There's something in the earth,
The promise of new birth,
A wakening of all living things
And the world is alive with bustling throng -
It is spring.

When the earth blossoms forth in glowing colours
And the new leaves glisten on the trees
And the air is alive -
Hear its voice singing out in the breeze.

There's something in the wind,
A stirring deep within,
A quickening that makes my heart sing
And the world is alive with hope reborn -
It is spring.

Rosemary Williams

OH! THAT UPLIFTING FEELING!

Oh! What is this wonderful, uplifting feeling?
Bright daylight and sunshine dazzles, I'm reeling!
Birds in the trees are calling and singing,
Love is in the air, to their mate they'll be winging.

Little green shoots are magically springing,
Bright yellow primroses were hiding, appearing,
Tall, golden daffodils stand erect, smile a greeting,
Each day new wonders, nature will be revealing.

Pulsating energy brings this springtime awakening,
It's all happening now, it is simply amazing.
Clocks move one hour forward, proof of spring arriving,
For a new image, new clothes folk will be striving.

This is a time of an explosion of giving,
Gifts for Mothers, for their devoted love and caring.
Mothering Sunday, a great family day of sharing,
Will someone somewhere be forgotten, I'm wondering?

Easter eggs arrive, new life is their meaning,
Shops fill their shelves, colourful boxes gleaming.
On farms hatching eggs are miraculously cracking,
Out of the shells, fluffy yellow chicks are popping!

Springtime is a time when miracles are happening,
Little white lambs born, soon seen jumping,
Humans when born lay in a cot just sleeping,
Progress first made, on all fours, just crawling!

Gone the dark winter when we tried hibernating,
Wrapped in woollies, cold, life so frustrating.
Gales and blizzards and earthquakes shaking,
Storms and floods, rivers rushing and rising,
Spring 2003 – finds a Gulf War looming!
Yet silently, spring brings that uplifting feeling!

S M Bush-Payne

SPRING

Everything blooming today and every day
The birds singing their praise in a new way
Early lambs in the field, exploring all around
Lambs are noisily looking, to see what can be found
Daffodils standing brightly, ablaze in the sun
Birds searching for food, around for their young
Rooks making their nests so high,
Up high in the boughs nearer the sky
Wind blowing through the trees
Swaying branches with the breeze
Spring is springing everywhere.

Marian Clark

SPRINGTIME

Cherry, may, lilac and laburnum set in blossomed glory,
The miraculous month of May unfolds her annual story.

The blackened trees overnight have gained verdant colour,
Nature's creation is reacting to a resurrection wonder.

Settled pigeons coo high aloft in coniferous trees
And lesser birds vie for a place in the foliage breeze.

At dawn they sing an introit from their choir stalls
But sleepy human heads respect not such early morning calls.

Roy Rudd

SPRING

March is now upon us
The month in which things change
It arrived with such a bang
But will leave unnoticed which is strange

At last a little sunshine
The spring is here again
I see it creeping through the clouds
In battle with the rain

The park is filled with colour
Spring flowers are growing fast
And all the hibernating animals
Are waking up at last

The winter nights are fading
Making way for more daylight
The clocks will soon go forwards
As the nights are getting bright

New lives are now beginning
In rivers, ponds and fields
Just one of nature's miracles
In which the springtime yields.

J L Preston

OUR GARDEN

The hedges around our garden are growing quite tall,
They need a good trim to keep them growing small.
The grass needs cutting, get the lawn mower out,
That needs a good clean and an oil can, thereabouts
So much to do, this time of the year,
It will be much easier after a glass of beer.
It's so nice to enjoy the taste, specially the fresh air,
Sitting out here in my favourite armchair.

I could spend all day sitting here with nothing to do,
Just watching my master doing these things for you.
I may have just four legs and a wagging tail,
But it's my garden to romp in, night and day, without fail.

Walter J Coleman

SPRINGTIME AT KIMMERIDGE BAY

Look at the sandpiper on the sandy foreshore,
Skittering in between the rocks and with a blest call,
Such a colourful thing,
And such a bright thing!
Stencilling its tiny footsteps,
They are like small rings,
Before the waves will wash them away once more.
And with lovely flapping sound
Of all the birds on the cliff tops,
Ledges - then suddenly they
Decide to fly away.
It is a grand sight of springtime
Being around the bay.
On a cloudless blue sky,
As you gaze upon the sea,
Happily for a short stay.
It is heaven to me!

'Sammy' Michael Davis

SPRING FAIRIES

The winter months are almost done
Spring will soon be in the air
And unbeknown to most of us
Spring fairies are everywhere.

They move around on silken wings
With only whispered sound
Raising crocuses and snowdrops
Out of the frozen ground.

Such beauty and such colour
Into our lives they bring
We should all be grateful
For these first signs of spring.

Still they are not finished
They have more work for many hours
Creating even more beauty
With the next stage of spring flowers.

Another task they undertake
And complete it with such ease
Is to put cloaks of green leaves
On winter's skeletal trees.

Any time you're out of doors
Try not to make a sound
And if you listen to the silence
You'll hear fairies all around.

No matter what the season
Or what time of the year
Fairies weave their magic
Just for us they're always here.

David Mentiply

CALCOT SPRING

At dawn my window opens on a flood of green;
A garden of dew-dream,
Whistling and calling with birdsong.
Bluebells tremble from damp clotted earth,
Lit from within by the newborn sun.
Orange crocuses turn tiger faces to the sky;
They drink the water-wobble of blue.
Van Gogh's sunflowers
Burst yellow on my lounge wall.
Eight daffodils bloom
From the throat of a cut glass vase.
Lucid morning light refracts
A crystal sweet-mix in a round glass bowl.
The sun speckles on my green jungle wall.
The spread of spring's parasol shelters all.

Charlotte Leather

SPRING IS ON THE WAY

I knew spring was on the way
When I opened my eyes today.
The sky was a beautiful blue,
Dark clouds, where are you?

The overnight rain had stopped,
Out of hiding the sun popped.
I decided to go out for a walk,
My neighbours wanted to talk.

Everyone had a smile on their face,
Happy to be part of the human race.
Soon people will be in the fresh air,
Throwing off clothes and woes without a care.

Working in the garden or washing the car,
Sitting outside with a nice cup of char.
That window has a smear on the glass
And I really must mow the grass.

Enjoying the first holiday of the year,
As once again Easter time is here.
A good excuse to have some fun,
To eat chocolate eggs or a hot cross bun.

Rosemary Davies

HERALDS OF SPRING

A really wonderful time of the year
Is when the aconites and snowdrops appear.
They form a carpet of yellow and white,
Which delights the eye with a beautiful sight.
Then the daffodils follow to give us cheer,
Heralding that once again spring is here.
Their bright yellow trumpets wave in the breeze,
Joined by the budding on shrubs and trees.
Each plant will grow and flower in season,
Each one has a purpose and a reason,
To respond to the elements, rain and sun,
All as God planned, and His will, will be done.

Vera Hankins

TURNAROUND

The thrush sings its romantic song
The robins flirt as they bob along
The snowdrops appear whiter than white
The tulip heads rear up overnight

The sights and sounds of spring
A smile to many these do bring
The buds appearing on the trees
The frosts now begin to cease

The warmth from the sun can be felt
As the snow is now forced to melt
The hilltops change from white to green
Oh, thankfully spring can definitely be seen.

Carol Whittaker

SPRINGTIME

The cold winter winds and frosty nights
Are beginning to fade and moving out,
And in their place the bulbs come through
Spring is here, the sky is blue.
The wind is light and the sun is warm,
Trees and hedges blooming leaves and thorns,
The grass is growing in God's good fields,
The sheep are lambing in the fields.
It's springtime for the birds as well,
Finding their mate and nesting in the dell,
The parks and gardens are coming through,
Daffodils, primroses, violets too,
So what a show God's done for you,
To look and have a wonderful view.

Ernest Edward Eady

SPRING

New life
Beneath the earth,
Stirs, rises to seek the sun
Warm, mellow, comforting. She wakes
Unfurls.

Green shoot
Peeps through the soil
The golden daffodil
Raises her face to greet the bright day.
Sleep over.

She basks
In the sunlight,
Feeling the breath of breeze
She sways, dances, joyful to rise
To live.

To hear
The birds singing
Cold, dark winter gone now
Bright, glorious gold, she lives again.
In spring.

Joan M Jones

SPRINGTIME, NATURE'S SEASON OF REVIVAL

After a long winter, everyone looks forward to spring,
People feel brighter, some even prompted to sing.
Crocuses and daffodils nodding gently in the breeze,
Leaves and blossom appearing on the trees.

Long walks in the country, watching the lambs,
Children playing, young mothers with prams.
Days lengthening rapidly, lots of sunshine,
Vegetables growing nicely, all in a line.

Spring mornings, birds singing sweetly in the trees,
Butterflies dancing, the hypnotic buzzing of bees.
Farmers in their fields, ploughing and sowing,
The cattle chewing grass, mooing and lowing.

Birds gathering materials, building their nests,
Flying to and fro all day with hardly a rest.
Frogspawn in ponds, floating in clumps,
Spring definitely lifts you out of the dumps.

New life all around, lots of new beginnings,
Mother Nature never loses, she's always winning.
Shrugging off winter's battle for survival,
Embracing spring's victory, a vibrant revival.

D I Muncaster

GREET THE DAY

Spring is live and still a time
Where animals and verdure
Greet a day!

Spring is garlanded in the still-
Present flowers and growth
Greet a day!

Spring still captured in the
Wintry night is present yet
Greet a day!

Spring harbours birth of animals
A time of youth and age to
Greet a day!

Spring knows the changing skies
And movement of the seas and stars
Must follow in the blacken'd night
Timeless in our climes to overcome
The swift apocalyptic ride in a climate variable to
Greet a day!

John Amsden

MOTHER NATURE

I sit on this hill and look for miles around,
I'm watching Mother Nature and listening to her sounds,
From the wind on my face to the beat in my heart,
I can't help thinking, *how did it all start?*
Watching fields full with lambs being born,
Seeing their mothers feed them and keeping them warm,
Observing them learn to stand and walk,
Listening to mother and new baby talk,
I'm watching Mother Nature at her best,
I'm seeing animals play then stop and rest,
Then I turn and see trees stretching up to the sky,
I can see flowers blooming and birds flying high,
I can see fish in the rivers that run so deep,
Watching animals drink, from field mice to sheep,
I'm watching Mother Nature looking after her own,
I know to be with Mother Nature means I'm never alone.

Karl A Hunter

GIFTS OF SPRING

'Oh, to be in England, now that April's here'
Is a line in Browning's poem, quoted far and near.
He epitomises in that poem
The unrivalled beauty of the spring,
It fills one's heart with joy and gladness
With the promise of lovely days it brings.

Spring is surely the best of all seasons,
Not just for its beauty, but for many reasons.
Following the dreary winter, it's so uplifting to see
The buds and glorious blossom appearing on many a tree.
Magnolias, laburnum and pretty flowering cherries,
A glimpse of summer and forerunners of autumn's berries.

High up in the trees, the birds begin to sing again,
Loving the springtime sunshine, undeterred by April rain.
Green shoots appear in gardens and fields,
Warmed by the sun, the frozen ground finally yields.
First come the snowdrops, delicate and white,
Followed by the crocus clothed in colours bright.
The wonderful sight of hundreds of daffodils
Is a much better medicine than doctor's pills,
All this beauty around us makes life worth living,
To enjoy these bountiful gifts Mother Nature is giving.

Jean Wood

HOPE PREVAILS

Dull and dreary winter
months have passed us by.
Finally, there is some hope
shimmering from the sky.

Subtle rays of sunshine,
evading the thick clouds,
dancing in between them,
dispersing those dark shrouds.

Glimmering streaks of lightness,
bringing tidings of worth,
raining on the snowdrops,
giving new hope on earth.

The grass is growing green.
New buds will soon be seen,
calves and lambs to be born
and the farmers can plant their seeds of corn.

Birds all in a flutter,
building nests in the gutter.
A sense of re-creation
as they look forward to a new generation.

New beginnings, new dreams,
spring is here at last,
bringing renewed energy and cheer,
now that winter's gloom is clear.

Eve McGrath

SPRING IS A BEAUTIFUL THING

After the cold and dark winter nights
Spring arrives with new delights
Flowers come alive
And wedding bells ring
Bees buzz round the hive
And the birds sing
Making a wonderful sound
Butterflies flutter all around
You can smell the spring air
Fresh and sweet
Juicy fruit is ripe and ready to eat
Love is in the air in the month of spring
That's why it's a beautiful thing.

Cassie Brown (15)

MY COMPANION

A wounded bird with broken limb
Comes daily to my windowpane.
Throughout the winter snow and rain
He hourly sings his haunting hymn;
He hops along and follows me,
The potting shed our mutual place,
Scraps are pecked without a trace,
His thanks, he whistles from the tree;
In rain and wind my songster knows
I work much faster, whistling low,
While little seedlings start to grow
And bolder now each day he grows;
Spring is here and flowers shoot
From the border and the hedge,
Still he sings from sunny ledge
And all the time new plants take root.

Norma Rudge

RUSTLE OF SPRING

Banks alight with bells of blue,
Campion, pink, of brilliant hue,
Clouds of hawthorn, pink and white -
Ever an enchanting sight.
Early orchis, fairy spire -
Pyramids of purple fire;
Scent of lilac, soft spring rain,
Laburnum's graceful, drooping chain;
Chestnut candles burn anew
Beneath a canopy of blue.
Apple blossom on the bough,
Copper Beech's fiery glow;
Hedges tipped with vivid green,
Surely God's hand can be seen?
Woolly lambs with plaintive bleat,
Daisy stars beneath one's feet;
Swallows screaming on the wing -
Welcome harbingers of spring.
Maypole dancing on the green . . .
Now, alas, too rarely seen;
But compensations yet abound -
Morris, Floral, still are found.
The fragrant hours fly by too soon
To usher in the month of June;
Then, as the long, hot days unfold . . .
Summer meadows, splashed with gold.

Elizabeth Amy Johns

EARLY ONE MORNING

One morning, two children had a surprise,
Though spring lambs expected, this news was not.
Their mouths fell open, they widened their eyes,
Mother bit her lip as Dad told them what
They would find if they ran to the stable.
They dashed there as fast as they were able.

For solemn faced, Dad had said, 'Overnight
Our horse has foaled. Now we've a baby horse . . .
You'll both want to see this wonderful sight.'
At the stable door, out of breath, of course,
They found their large horse with long tail and mane,
Moving to munch hay, again and again.

Disappointed, they ran back crying, *'Dad!*
Someone must have stolen the baby horse!
It's gone! Phone the police! It's really bad!'
Dad grinned at them, 'Hush! Your voices are hoarse,
You forget . . . our horse is a stallion.
Foaled? April fools! For he could not have done!'

Later, when Dad led their horse to the trough,
Before he dropped his maned head down to drink,
His horse-face glanced at them - and seemed to laugh -
While the children did not know what to think.
Last year, they'd made their parents April fools,
This morning, someone had just changed the rules . . .

Chris Creedon

THE PROMISE OF SPRING

The dainty little snowdrop,
Just tinged with delicate green,
It adorns the whole of the countryside,
It's a joy where'er you've been.
They are out in their abundance,
A reminder of the spring,
Soon other flowers will follow
As we hail the season . . . spring.

J Mary Kirkland

THE LITTLE RED ROSE

A red rose in the garden
All on its own
No one to nurture her
She grows alone

She's filled up with pride
Her head is held high
Admiring the stars
That waltz in the sky

When the dawn breaks
And the rain starts to fall
She is pleased. It will help
Her branches grow tall

When the sun shines
She turns her head round
Weeds all about her are
Growing out of the ground

The day isn't nice it's
Very dismal and gloom
But she doesn't care because
Her buds are in bloom.

A Whyte

JOURNEY INTO SPRING

Snowdrops
These tiny drops of pure delight
Their joyful message bring
A gentle sign of nature's might -
The great awakening.

Crocuses
So cheekily with faces bright
Defying frost and snow
A colour scheme mixed with delight
To bid the winter go.

Daffodils
Gay golden trumpets without a sound
Silently heralding
This new-born nature all around
The miracle of spring.

Primroses
And then perchance beneath our feet
Amidst the woodland shade
A purity so rare to meet
There tenderly displayed.

Bluebells
With simple splendour spread around
Nestling beneath the trees
No carpet ever graced the ground
So well designed to please.

Blossom
Bewitched by beauty, tho' I vow
More than a magic dream
Enchantment borne upon the bough
Proud party of nature's scheme.

Springtime
To field and footpath, hedge and hills
Woodland and gardens too
A wonderland alive with thrills
Springtime returns anew.

Cecil J Lewis

WHAT IS SPRING?

S hoots of green emerging bravely
   from under their brown coverlet of soil.
P rimroses nestling on a sunny, mossy bank,
   their pale yellow faces welcoming the warmth.
R abbits venturing to sample juicy, dew-drenched
   grass, nibbling with great rapidity.
I ncreasing birdsong as nests are lovingly lined
   to shelter the hungry fledglings.
N ew-born lambs frolicking in the fields
   within sight of their munching mother.
G reen grass, green leaves of varying hue,
   gently portraying life anew.

This is spring.

Daphne F Murphy

LIFE IS BEGINNING

Oh yes. Yes, it's here
My favourite season of the year.
Life's little bud on branch of tree
Waiting to burst open at being free,
Bulbs peeping from underground
Pushing stretching without a sound.
Dark dismal mornings have gone at last,
Young spring lambs jumping ever so fast,
Young birds chirping, what's the big deal?
Mum has gone to get them a morning meal.
You look around and life has begun,
This beautiful sight is for everyone.
The smell is so fresh that is in the air,
Just treat it with respect, it's only fair.
Spring is the time for love in the air,
Couples walking hand in hand,
Oh, don't they make a lovely pair?
Rabbits hopping in the grass,
They stop, look around, till the humans pass.
Nature is such a beautiful thing,
No wonder the birds sit in the trees
And sing and sing.
It must have taken God some time
To develop this scene
With all its beauty and shades of green.

Rosalind Jennings

THIS WORLD

He walked along the wildflower-strewn path
That meandered by the river,
The flashing colours of a kingfisher in flight
He saw, reflected in the water's shimmer.

Warm sunlight bathed his arms and face
And he smelt the fresh-mown grass,
How glorious looked the woods and fields
Of nature's beauty unsurpassed.

The country sounds fell on his ears
With the raucous cries of crows
And the woodpecker's incessant knocking
To pick its food from fresh made holes.

Cotton wool clouds scud across the deep blue sky
Casting shadows across the sun,
With fish splashing as they leap for flies
And young hares jink and run for fun.

This world is a very beautiful place,
With scenes breathtaking to the human eye
And the great mammals swim in the oceans deep,
All this belongs to you and I.

Tony Pitt

SPRING 2003

It's hard to take pleasure in springtime
In the year 2003.
The mind tends to dwell on the future,
If future there's going to be!

The sun *will* come up tomorrow,
But shall we be here to see?
The threats against us are very real
Made indiscriminately.

We'd like to greet each morning
With a lift of the heart each day
But if all we will have is the mourning,
Our summer will seem far away!

So as the season slips from winter
As the trees wake from their sleep,
Pray to whatever gods you know
In safety our world to keep!

Joyce M Jones

SHOWER SENSE

Hardly even noticed at first. Then, sharply felt!
The tiny infrequent spatters that grew to a pelt.
Running for a vacant doorway in which to hide,
I stared at the heavens and impatiently sighed.
But my heart, a passionate lover of the flower,
Soon ruled my head in favour of this spring shower.
And with my refreshed outlook on today's gloom,
I can see to the near future - a summer in bloom!

Donna June Clift

SPRINGTIME

When March winds are blowing
And green tips are showing,
It's hard to remember our care,
When spring is here,
When full streams are gushing
And new buds are flushing,
And strange songs are heard in the air,
It's hard to remember the grey
Of December darkness,
The snow and the cold,
We're too busy dreaming - of sunshine
A-gleaming and trumpets of daffodil gold.

Our gloomy obsessions and
Morbid depressions are blown,
Helter-skelter away, our mopings
And groanings, our grumblings
And groanings are silenced;
Dark thoughts kept at bay . . .
When March winds come out to play
And bright rays come pouring through
Windows that look to the sun,
You can't go round crying
When nature is trying
To get you to join in the fun.

R Vincent

WINTER TURNS TO SPRING

snowfall heavy ice-blue
reproduced a Christmas-card view
the biting wind swirled one-foot drifts
overhanging banks, bridges makeshift

the flooded fields iced skating rinks
into which each footstep sinks
cracking under body weight
not the place to slide or skate

thawing februar' brought twitching noses
in tussock grass, dormant primroses
and rummaging on hazel boles,
hibernating mammals desert their holes

on hedgerow leafless, buds start to form
above a carpet flowing of white corm
badgers forage food outside their sett
bracken branch, bluebell-scented couchette

bird food sources declining fast
grass, chickweed, groundsel their scant repast
sparrows, wrens, robins pair in twos
as lengthening days come into view

winter aconite open in strengthening sun
yellow pendant catkins lambs' tails fine spun
osier shoots bursting forth with green corn camomile
as early spring mornings manage a smile

Brian Strand

SPRING IS

When brave white snowdrops and golden daffodils first appear,
It's that special time, glorious spring is finally here.
Like morning dew our hearts and spirits are fresh and bright,
As evening stretches, giving that long awaited welcome light.

Robins, sparrows and dappled thrushes singing with exuberance
                                            and might,
Hedgerows, trees and bushes laden with nutritious buds of delight.
Baby lambs, some caramel, cream, snowy-white or black as night,
Frolic and frisk, then skip in fright at warning bleats to stay in sight.

Mr Mad March Hare spars and shadow-boxes with his best pal,
Wonders should he go for a run? Then thinks, *Oh yes, I shall.*
Happy Easter bunnies joyfully take a bow and gladly venture out,
New-born chicks pick, dab, dandle or jauntily jig about.

The sun is out! Yet snow showers still boldly come and go
What shall we wear - coat or sun top? It's really hard to know.
There's a spring in our steps, any mountain we can climb,
Love is in the air, smiles are everywhere, springtime is so divine.

Angela Moore

BLESSED INTERVAL

Silence - watching a slower moving river
Seated in God's sun, so warm and friendly
In balmy air and sweet gentle breeze.
Dignified now those white swans, and ducks more graceful,
Washing and preening, unhurried and unthreatened,
Their time - like mine just now - to simply be.

O Father of love - provided space you knew we needed
So beautifully healing the pace of human life,
While receiving this little refreshment, no need to concentrate
In these shallow waters of happy and rested emotions.
In this safe environment brought closer to security,
Yes Father - now I recognise myself again.

Here held in this little holiday of value
Draw closer to the creator of all that is around me,
Loving this welcome stillness of my soul
And the spiritual love within can awaken from its sleep.
The aeroplane above white clouds hums contentedly,
Listen to accompaniment of Heaven deepening my peace,
Feeling part of nature now - where man belongs,
Trees and bushes are like friends who understand.

In this holy place of rest - content to be a little sleepy,
Meandering by, young lovers arm in arm,
Indicating things of heartfelt interest and charm.
No need for now - I know - to speak, or do,
Just float on this sacred level of my retreat.

My mind, childlike, meditates on smaller delights I see,
My healing body loves it all - and tells me so.
Perhaps the creator's angel holds me in caress awhile?
Unfettered by the busy play of life's advances.

It is - the interval,
And I am - blessed,
And I will - return thankfully again for more.

Don Harris

SPRING 2003

It's spring 2003.
The war has just begun
In Iraq with its desert warfare,
Fierce sandstorms and blazing sun.
Even thunderstorms with pouring rain.
The landscape turns to mud.
Soldiers struggle to release lorries and tanks,
Careful of enemy gunfire and heavy missile thud.
A weary, mud-stained soldier
Dreams of home as he takes a rest.
Thoughts of daffodils and starry nights,
A time when Mother Nature is at her best.
Will he walk again in fields wet with dew,
See the hillsides purple with heather?
When tiny lambs play and baby birds learn to fly,
Will he and his girlfriend spend next spring together?
To walk hand in hand where the primroses bloom,
To run through green trees, calling her name.
A whistling bullet disturbs his thoughts, moves him on,
In 2003, spring is not the same.

Joy Cooke

AND SUDDENLY IT'S SPRING

Last week it seemed that winter would never end -
The wind blew from the north and from the east and
The black, bare branches of the sycamore
Looked dead; birds sat huddled in the bush
Outside the window, feathers plumped up against the cold,
Feeding hungrily on the food put out for them.
Everything depressing, dark and bleak.

And now, today, suddenly it's spring.
Fat buds have appeared on the trees, waiting to explode
Into the fresh green leaves of early summer.
Primroses and bright celandine grow along the hedge
And yellow daffodils and dandelions bedeck the verge.
Bird song fills the air, nest boxes are inspected by tits,
Sparrows, chaffinches and the cheeky robin,
And jackdaws build their nests, noisily, in the chimney pots.
In the warm and welcome sun, the first flowers open on the camellia
And bees buzz happily in the azalea bush.
In the evenings the blackbird's wondrous song is heard
Filling the garden as night falls.
Everywhere new life is appearing and hope is born anew.
What joy there is in nature's re-awakening. Winter is gone -
And suddenly it's spring.

Ann Linney

SPRING IN THE AIR

Winter's snow and frost and ice
Have all passed away in a thrice
Gentle spring has come to greet us
With mild breezes and no fuss
Sunlight shoots golden light
And shines through the trees with all its might.
Birds can be heard singing in the trees
And quietly buzzing around are the busy bees.
One by one the bright flowers appear as in a fashion show
The trees are turning green with new leaves so rare
And are waving their branches in the cool air.
The lambs are frisking in the meadows green
Watched by the shepherd who works as a team
But spring's sunny days don't last I fear -
We'll have to wait another year.

Margaret Kelly

SPRING HAS SPRUNG

Now that winter has at last lost its peek
Blackbirds will soon begin to speak
With their harsh, noisy rattles of alarm
With notes full of cheerful charm.

The mistle thrush listens, on the treetops high
With her characteristic notes, as she flies, through the sky
With her flute-like repetition of similar chatter
Soon she will join in, with the blackbird's natter.

Oh how wonderful to hear, such different tones
While the blue tit sings sweetly on her own
Her high-pitched call notes, followed with a trill
Such melodies are heard, as the fresh air seems still.

Tulips are in full bloom, with their fragrance and graces
When once golden daffodils, showed their yellow faces
While bluebells are gathered once again
Even through the warmth of the showery rain.

While trees bloom out with lilac and lime
The notes of the church bells sweetly chime
Such merriment sounds far away, but loud and clear
Such a contrast makes the day, so full of cheer.

The enchantment the countryside knows, on a clear day
While squirrels come out of the willows, to play
Chasing each other, around the blossom of the trees
While the leaves whisper, to the whistle, of the breeze.

When winter is behind us, and spring has sprung,
Till twilight appears, the birds rest, when day is done.

Jean McGovern

EMERGENCE

I had confiscated dreams,
exquisite spring experience,
for, when winter growls, it seems
Elysium is mere pretence.
I had shut away motif
impermanent, of priceless worth;
arbours triumphant, in leaf,
I pictured, glorifying Earth,
grandiose, theatrical
treasured, free performance staged,
thrush and blackbird lyrical,
voices stored whilst tempest raged.
Patiently I queued for more,
in arctic reverie restrained;
eventually I saw
again sweet April showers rained.
Out comes cramped, denied idea,
the bent and crumpled, starved response;
liberated life draws near
and I am happy all at once.

Ruth Daviat

AT LAST THE SPRING HAS SPRUNG

My favourite time of year is here
The air seems new, so fresh and clear
With early bird song in your ear
At last the spring has sprung

New life bursting all around
Lambs in fields, they jump and bound
Daffodils cover woodland ground
At last the spring has sprung

Days out with the family
In the country, or by the sea
Enjoy the sun, it's yours for free
At last the spring has sprung

Although some days can turn out wet
It won't last long, so don't you fret
The clocks go forward, don't forget
At last the spring has sprung.

George Wilford

SPRING

Spring is such a special time
Sunshine, April showers
Green shoots peeping through the earth
Buds on trees and flowers

A feeling of expectancy
As nature wakes from her winter rest
Birds singing high above
And busy building nests

A sense of fresh beginnings
Stirring all around
People wearing friendly smiles
Lambs gambolling on the ground

Everyone seems brighter
Less loath to leave their bed
Gardeners sharpening up their tools
For the tasks that lie ahead

We can forget the winter gloom
The cold, dark days are past
The world seems a much nicer place
For spring is here at last.

May Morrott

THE YELLOW PANSY

It seems such a while since I planted them
all those many months ago.
Exposed to all the weathers,
wind, rain and snow.

The hanging basket protecting them
has swung from here and there.
Leaves fluttering flirtatiously
plain, green and bare.

No bright, pretty petals
nodding their heads with glee.
At least not until today,
when I saw one wink at me.

It was as bright as a sherbet lemon
so sharp and clearly formed.
Alone in perfect wonder
so proud to be born.

Despite our darkened times
nature never ceases to amaze.
We have such pleasure in its company
in so very many ways.

Lynn Craig

TWILIGHT

As shadows fall across the tired earth,
The evening sun lies bleeding in the west
And birds upon the wing fly home
So swiftly to their nest.
The flowers all their perfumed petals close
And meadows weep with glistening dew.
The trees stand tall and slowly sway
As twilight steals the end of day.
Soon now the sky a different colour takes
As night feels sorry for the earth below,
A velvet blue drips diamonds like a crown,
Behold the stars, the eyes of night peer down
And moonlight's beams in a veil of lace
Fall softly on the Earth's quiet face.

Christina Lily Young

NATURE'S NECESSITIES

There's a place that I like to go,
It's deep within the woods,
There I can witness all of nature's necessities,
The flowers and the buds.

In the spring, baby lambs are born
And plants begin to bloom,
Grass sways and flowers open
Under the light of the moon.

Then in the summer, the sun shines down
Upon oceans clear and deep,
While children play and laugh all day
In the sand found on the beach.

In the autumn the leaves turn to gold
And from the trees they fall like fire.
They dance upon the gentle breeze,
Falling first lower then higher.

In the winter the ground is covered in snow
And icicles hang from the trees.
Singing its song in the frost-covered land,
The robin helps to please.

I sit in this place every day
And gaze upon the sight
Of Mother Nature's masterpiece
That fades into the night.

Gemma King

KETTLE ROBIN

Have you found a kettle robin;
Lying on the ground,
Somewhere you can settle often,
Flying round and round,
Underneath a hawthorn tree
Sprouts a near-white gown,
Shady leaf and early bee;
Spout is facing down.

Dunnocks now are seen in pairs,
Mistle builds a nest,
Blackbirds putting on great airs,
Little time to rest;
Soon the fevered gathering,
Earthworm, bug and snail,
To their children offering,
Tiny mouths prevail.

Have you found a kettle-robin,
Wren is passing by,
Low within a metal casing;
Looking with her eye,
I can't save you - or your young,
Predators come near,
Trusting they shall be among
Visitors next year . . .

Tom Ritchie

WHAT IS DONE IS DONE

If you plant your seeds
And nurture them with care,
But still there is no harvest,
Please do not despair.

For as the farmer in his fields
Has done what he should do,
Should the harvest be destroyed,
This I say to you.

Like the freak of nature
That took his crop from him,
It's not by his own hand,
The farmer knows within.

So look to the future,
For the time will come,
When you can sow your seeds again,
For what is done is done.

C S Cyster

THE GARDENER

He ties the tall chrysanthemums
He binds their stems with care
My father's work is never done
I see him always there

He often talks of days gone by
I see another face
As eyes of youthful calculus
Light up an empty space

I see his fingers carefully plant
The seed into the ground
In his eye, he sees it grow
And flower all around

He is a silent gardener
Of thoughtful reverie
The baccy tin of Old Holborn
Lies planted on his knee
Here, fingers furl a rizzly white
As tongue licks down its way
Of quiet pause - and firelight
And smoke of curling grey

At times like this - when stormy nights
Beat loudly with their spill
And lightning crosses all the sky
And darkness brings its dim
I think then of the gardener - I wonder of his work
I know whatever storm my bring
The gardener will not shirk

And yes, I see the gardener
I see him bending still
Beside the clouds that overcast
Their shapes on Heathered Hill
His fingers tie a memory - of stems that never fray
A gardener's work is never done
It goes on - day by day.

Diana Mullin

THE MONTH OF MARCH

March is a month of change and movement,
We look to spring and weather improvement.
On the first we remember St David, the patron saint of Wales,
The people also think of leeks and daffodils!
March hares are a rare sight today,
We call them 'mad' because of their play.
Some weeks of the month are in the season of Lent,
God's people try to fast and be penitent.
Mothering Sunday is thought of too,
With cards and gifts in our shopping to do.
Easter eggs on sale in the shops now,
Can we afford them? We find it somehow!
Although March is a busy month today,
Try to find time to rest and pray.

Joyce Hallifield

SPRING HAS SPRUNG

It made me think that spring is here
When I saw the birds suddenly appear.
Amused to see them splashing about in the bird bath,
First one got in, then the other, what a laugh!

Green foliage coming up from the bulbs,
Next, so many colours flowing from the bud.
A sky such a delicate blue,
So amazing when the sun comes through.

Nature is a marvellous thing,
As everything starts to grow, the first sign of spring.
It lifts our spirits now winter has gone,
So we can look forward to the summer on.

Evelyn M Harding

SPRING

Spring's arrived again,
A season that brings out the best.
Daffodils and tulips peep through the soil,
After a long winter's rest.

People begin to smile.
They even stop to say hello.
Days are longer, more relaxed
With time to take things slow.

Trees burst with new life,
Buds ready to explode,
Birds wait in anticipation
For foliage to shelter their abode.

Awake to the sound of songbirds,
How sweetly they sing.
There's nothing can compare
To the amazing events of spring.

Anne Leeson

SPRING

Spring is when the sunrise brings
A bright and early dawn,
Spring is when the gardener's out
To mow a thickening lawn.

Spring is when the nesting birds
Are chirping high in trees,
Spring is when the blossom scent
Allures the honeybees.

Spring is when a range of buds
Develop into flowers,
Spring is when the burgeoning sun
Accompanies April showers.

Spring is when the daylight hours
Extend in longer days,
Spring is when folk venture out
To catch those first warm rays.

Spring brings eggs and hot cross buns
For holidays expected,
Spring brings new life bursting forth
From deadwood resurrected.

Ivan S Thomas

SPRING FEVER

Winter slips into spring
On a cushion of wild primrose flowers
With the lengthening of the days
And increasing daylight hours

A welcoming warmth is felt
From the rays of the struggling sun
March hares and madness magnify
This reckless spirit of fun

Birds flitter and flutter around
They've a family of chicks to rear
Eagerly courting their ladies
Enticing them ever near

Nature adorns the countryside
Casting off winter's gloom
Trees thicken and cast shadows
While the lilac bursts into bloom

Winter is soon forgotten
As the land warms up and dries
Spring unveils her beauty
Before our wondering eyes

There's a comforting, familiar pattern
That happens every year
But still we watch with wonder
For the primrose to appear

Every spring we have renewal
Nature never gets it wrong
From the stirring of the earthbound roots
To the bird's melodic song.

Jackie Johnson

SPRING

March came in so peaceful
The earth will soon be warm
Spring is around the corner
The lambs will soon be born.

When as the earth gets warmer
And our flowers start to grow
We say goodbye to Jack Frost
And his icicles and snow.

We are always glad for April
And all the warm, bright sun
That's the time we always know
That spring has really sprung.

The birds welcome this time of year
When it's warm beneath the wing
And welcome are the mornings
When you hear the blackbirds sing.

Maurice P Oliver

SPRING

Invigoration, expectation are the feelings that come to mind
As the days grow slowly longer and the weather milder and more kind
To watch the miracle of the rebirth
As the sun warms up a frozen earth
Wondrously green shoots appear so small
You marvel at buds forming on trees so tall
Along come the snowdrops all so brave, dressed in green skirts
                                            and tops of white,
Then primroses, tulips, daffodils, who dance in delight
Nodding their heads, yellow trumpets glowing, so eager to please,
This way and that in tune with the breeze,
They lift up our spirits, such joy to behold
And tell us that springtime is coming, all ready to unfold
Its beauty in colours aspiring belief
In gambolling new lambs, trees bursting green leaves,
Blue skies and sunshine, white clouds not grey,
Soon the boats sailing way out in the bay.
People more cheerful being out and about,
Forgetting the strictures of winter no doubt,
Joyously feeling the need to spring-clean,
Reacting to nature as it's always been.
Bluebells carpet the woodland as a walk we take,
Ducks, drakes and swans glide by on the lake.
Nature awakening to the call of spring,
All things responding to the delight that she brings.

Marjorie Leyshon

SPRINGTIME

Blossom on bushes and nearby trees
Glistening, gleaming, sparkling seas

Hundreds of animals are being born
With the strong, fresh smell of a newly-cut lawn

A great shining sun in the sky
And the often buzz of a passing fly

People all around in a T-shirt and shorts
Everyone thinking summery thoughts

Cars with open sunroofs, sunlight streaming in
When you take a deep breath the cold air is thin

Longer days and shorter nights
On breezy days you see flying kites

Brighter colours are worn today
And we still have summer

Hip, hip, hooray!

Richard Freeman (10)

SPRING PUTS ON ITS COAT OF MANY COLOURS

God's silent messengers of spring captivate and delight my heart
And I gaze enraptured at the wonderful display of colour that
Decks the meadows, woodlands and parks.
My heart skips a beat as I lovingly greet the season of spring,
Glorious spring with outstretched arms.
I feel overwhelmed and full of joy
For I long to be caressed by their delicate charms.
Mother Nature proudly presents her bounteous offerings
And happily announces the arrival of spring.
An aura of mystery and power holds me spellbound as
Colours sparkle and dance like precious jewels in a ring.
The law of nature is renewed and the warmth of the sun
Is welcomed after the long, dreary days of winter.
Prayers of gratitude and joy flood my heart and I feel one
And a part of this marvellous bonanza.
How can one not help but stand and stare at such perfect splendour,
Without being aware of God's eternal love?

Spring flowers enchant me and all God's creatures awaken
Within me feelings of strong emotion.
A badger on the lane out foraging with it's young
Lifts my spirits with a cry of jubilation.
A baby rabbit separated from its parent and wandering about lost,
Arouses feelings of trepidation.
The birds herald spring with their early morning chirping
Happy to have survived frosty nights and near starvation.
Spring is a wonderful time on the farm when
Long awaited lambs and foals bring excitement and much interest.
The animals are very special and dear to me
And with the season of spring, I feel richly immersed.

Elizabeth Myra Crellin

ASPECTS OF SPRING

As rain splashes down on a late winter's day
It seems that spring is still far away.
Although snowdrops have shown us their helmets of white
And bird song begins with the dawn's first light.

Soon blossom will appear on the trees once again
And daffodils' golden trumpets proclaim,
'Spring is coming - spring is here,'
The warm sunny days we will greet with a cheer.

However, this feeling may well disappear
As the thought of spring-cleaning becomes very clear.
With curtains and covers the washing line loaded
Furniture polished and cupboards are tidied.

One look in the wardrobe casts gloom on my reason
There's nothing to wear to bring joy to the season.
So, that's quite enough dusting and quite enough mopping
With a clean home in order, I'm off to go shopping!

Meryl

SPELLBOUND

Shafts of sunbeams shine through the trees,
shimmering, sparkling on the ground,
the sky alive with birds and bees,
delight the sense of sight and sound.

The gentle murmur of the stream,
rippling over the stones and weeds,
sunlight making the water gleam,
sycamore trees shedding their seeds.

Spreading wide each gossamer wing,
rainbow colours caught in the sun,
heading towards their toadstool ring
the fairies gather one by one.

Bluebell and rose and celandine,
dogwood, hogwart, cobweb and moss,
primrose, lily and columbine,
tiny bodies covered in floss.

Seated around the king and queen
resplendent in their green and gold,
enchantment spreading over the scene,
spellbound, bewitched, since times of old.

Tinkling voices blown by the breeze,
laughing, playing, never a care,
flying together through the trees,
once more the toadstool ring is bare.

A Odger

THE DAFFODIL

January sees a sprout
A little head poking out

February sees them grow
And the nectar starts to flow

March will see them standing proud
Yellow trumpets form a crowd

April brings yet another shower
'Tis the end of this lovely flower

May will see them wither and brown
It's time to lay their tired heads down

June will see them go to bed
Do not worry, they're not dead.

Peter Tilson

WEST COUNTRY WEATHER

We told you, didn't we - it was so?
From Dartmoor down to Plymouth Hoe;
We were, really, not being clever
When we said that we'd have weather!

From the Arctic to the tropics
It dominated - 'favourite' topics;
And, studying the birds of feather,
We were certain we'd have weather!

It came upon us - very sudden!
Even before the trees were 'buddin'!
Well before the Scottish heather,
Came the proof that we'd have weather!

Sometimes cold and sometimes hot,
And it rained too! Quite a lot!
Filling up the Tamar river,
Proving that - we're having weather!

It froze us stiff, it burned us dry,
It made us sometimes want to cry!
And though we dressed ourselves in leather,
We still experienced - the weather!

Rain, hail, sleet or snow
We tell you now - we told you so!
Even though, you thought that never
We could ever have - such weather!

R Bissett

THE LILY LEAVES

The moorhen with her dainty tread
Goes walking on the lily leaves,
Which shining green or russet red,
Seem like a land where fancy weaves.

The water shades are inky-blue
With silver bubbles floating through,
A little kingdom for the fish
Who idly near the surface rest
And glimpse our world from underneath
The lily leaves and moorhen's breast

Then rise to catch a passing fly
Or breathe the bubbles floating by.

Liz Osmond

My Garden

I love my garden when spring is here
With daffodils and pansies
A mass of colour blooming there
Among the trees, with crocuses
And roses of all shades growing round the lawn.
A clump of violets hiding behind the bushes
and the scented smell of lavender at dawn.
In the distance, a twittering bird is heard,
Such peace surrounds the garden that I love,
A stillness in the air, tranquillity at its best,
The sun shining down from up above,
Heaven sent, a perfect paradise.

R P Candlish

DON'T WORRY - BE HAPPY

Early morning sunshine,
The birds sweetly sing.
Little dog
Pads her paws
As if the day
Were spring.
Yesterday
It rained so.
Tomorrow
Winds may blow,
But as long as
We are happy,
A smile
We will
Show!

Lyn Sandford

NEW LIFE

Bird emerges from the shell
Pecking its way to the light,
Stretching wing, standing well,
What a truly wondrous sight!

From our mother's womb we're born,
Filling lungs, breathing alone,
From warm and safe place we're torn,
Fate we must never bemoan.

Light and life and love surround,
Another life has begun,
Parents, children, now are bound
Together, they are just one.

So keep the bond strong always,
From their flesh and blood we're made,
Love and honour all your days,
Hold head high, be not afraid.

Suzanne Joy Golding

WHAT MADE ME LOVE WORDS?
(The late John Clare)

The literary world named John 'Peasant Poet'.
Born in 1793, the son of a labourer
Wish I could go back in time and be there
Fell in love with 'John Clare' when reading 'The Eternity of Nature'
His beautiful poetry, country scenes
Places I wish to have seen.
Countryside he did roam
Alone, where nature is overgrown
Beside the molehills he did think
Listening to bird life, chirp and sing.
Wild flowers, morning pleasant walks
Clover blossoms, red and tawny white
Strong scented with summer's warm delight
The joy of morning's lovely hours
Amongst woodlands' opening flowers.
John Clare - are you still there?
Gazing on nature's scenes
That seem to smile

John Clare - The Caring Poet

THIS MEMORY

Standing by the rushing river,
Baited, ready to deliver,
Sounds and sights and hope as ever,
Tend to make me start to quiver,
Firmly holding rod and reel,
Waiting for a trout or eel,
Such adrenalin I feel,
This is living, this is real,
Here last year in early May,
Such a whopper got away,
I hope he's still in there today,
Things won't always go his way,
Everything is going fine,
Early sunbeams start to shine,
Something nudges at the line,
Easy now, he'll soon be mine,
Quickly sensing something wrong,
Off he surges, deep and long,
Now he's leaping high and strong,
The reel sings out its happy song,
Finally his strength gives out,
He's a fighter, there's no doubt,
What a prize, a lovely trout!
Now get the net and lift him out,
I'll remember when I'm grey,
This fine fish and this fine day,
Here, my mind will always stray,
This memory won't fade away.

Matthew L Burns

THE HAVEN

A garden captured inside a wall
As beauty is displayed for all
Exhibits fresh amid the bloom
As variety reaps and states its room

A sunflower stood tall and grand
With memories of its sun-drenched land
Carnations sold in many a spray
With colours galore in vast array

The daffodil, among its folk
A spring repeat; with a yellow yolk
Romantic choice, a perfect rose
Its petals caressed to keep its pose

This sanctuary for vision and scent
A rainbow scene with an outdoor vent
An escape for all; you're free to glide
So find your garden and step inside.

Kerry Feild

BUTTERFLIES

Beauteous butterfly, butterfly
Flutter by, flutter by,
How you flit from flower to flower
Up on high or lower.
With brilliantly-coloured translucent wings
Dazzling concentric rings.
Red admiral and painted lady
in sun and spots shady
See clouded yellows, peacocks too
That dance for me and you.
Once were caterpillar, larvae grown
Now beauty of your own
You move on south when autumn arrives
Leaving us empty skies
But what, alas, is your fate in store
Just pinned fast to a board.

Terry Daley

SAVED FROM A FIERY FURNACE

No palette could paint the colours of tonight's skies,
To compare a breathtaking moonlight or sunset would be compromise,
The red, orange, gold and yellow of the forest fire is a backdrop,
To compelling viewing, as from foot to foot we hop.

The forest is on fire, it's brought panic everywhere,
Scamper you creatures of the forest, scamper if you dare,
This roaring fire is raging, devouring all in its path,
Will there be survivors in this aftermath?

Sparks mimic shooting stars and sound like staccato music,
While twigs and bush burn and crackle, adding to the classic,
The howling winds deafen us like an unknown instrument,
Just like a tempestuous sea, with a vicious temperament.

Trees are falling as the earth becomes a carpet of ashes
As grime and dirt and dust stick to our eyelashes,
Our nostrils are filled with the smell of burning and soot,
Which blackens us all over, from head to foot.

The fire and heat is intense beyond any refining furnace,
We have no technology to put it in a harness,
The cries of exhausted creatures turn into whimpering sighs,
Is there any saving grace in the river flowing by?

Look, look, there is Mother Deer and baby in the water,
They seem transfixed, are they looking for husband and father?
In this one moment they must flee for their lives,
The heat is intense, yes, under the water they dive.

Baby deer follows Mum to the water's edge
And into the arms of the fireman who then makes a pledge,
'You are safe my frightened ones, off to the sanctuary,
Be assured if we see Mr Deer, he'll know just where you will be.'

Barbara Jermyn

A LOCAL RESIDENT

I have a little garden, it backs onto a park
The bottom end is shaded by some trees that make an arch
We have a local resident that lives beneath the ground
A vixen and her little cubs that love to play around
I often leave some food around when days and nights are cold
And love to watch them eat it, though I'm very often told
It isn't very proper to feed a starving fox
But I don't care what people say and neither does the fox
To me, I get great pleasure in helping who I can
It doesn't really matter if it's animal or man
We're, after all, God's creatures
Who have a right to live
And after all is said and done
It's better for to give
A little help to others who are harried every day
By evil meaning people in every dreadful way.

R T Gough

NATURE PREVAILS

Big JCBs and dumper trucks,
Digging the earth and shifting the muck,
Building houses everywhere, without a thought or care
For the small animals and birds nesting there,
Nature must prevail.

Soon there's quite a large estate,
All very modern and up-to-date,
They plant the gardens with trees once more,
Small shrubs, and bushes to the fore,
And nature will prevail.

The birds and squirrels start to drift back in,
To habitats new, but something is lacking,
The rabbits and field mice have not yet returned,
But the people have already learnt,
That nature will prevail.

Marjorie Cripps

JUST A TREE

Proud it has stood there through the years
Now sheds its leaves like falling tears
Men have come to cut it down
Silent it waits; there is not a sound
Many passed by since its creation
Only a few watch the cremation
Firelight lighting up their face
In my life an empty space
Some would say it is just a tree
But it seemed more like a friend to me.

Ivy Dixon

CALCULATING RAIN

The calculating rain now falls
O'er arid landscapes. Pays no calls
As more rich earth the sun's harsh rays do bleach
Which begs the rainfall now itself to reach.
But it ignores the desert's dying pleas:
Too busy filling distant, far-off seas.
So children die, along with their despair
But not with food and water - nothing's there.
Weak cries for help fall on rain's empty ears
For nothing's here but dry and dusty fears.
The calculating rain refuses, still, to fall
And answers not our desperate, thirsty call.

Hazel Mills

THE ALLEYWAY

Dried mummified dog dirt
The strong stench of cat squirt
Papier-mâché debris
Cans and cartons set free
Old rubble and broken bricks
Lost tree boughs and deadened sticks
But in it all nature played
A swathe on the landscape it had laid
There were nettles and stingers all amuck
Defiant golden dandelions amidst the ruck
And hedge bindweed sneaked and crept
Amongst the rubbish that we had left
Yellow common ragwort shyly lifted its crown
Embarrassed at the surroundings where it lay down.

Gail Sturgess

WHAT ABOUT THE REST OF US?

Brown leaf wet from rainy dew
Scattered around
The cold and stony crazy paving blue
Close breeze
Taking breath away
To the northern flights
Of blue tits
Robin, sparrow, tucked
Beneath their nest
Hibernate, go, go
Wishing we could all come
Come to join the flock
Feathered army.

E A Triggs

NATURE

Flowing streams that tumble down, going who knows where,
breezes whisper in your ear, and gently lift your hair,
Sun that warms you as you sit, in fields of shades of green,
life is all around you, so much can be seen,
Birds all busy on the wing, honeybees in flight,
butterflies amongst the flowers, dancing water sprite,
Hedgerows busy guarding nests, chirping sounds ring clear,
a rabbit runs along the bank, then it too disappears,
A spider spins a web of lace, upon the swaying stalks,
while ants are busy at their work, miles upon miles they walk,
A four-leaf clover rarely seen, is somewhere in this place,
buttercups and daisies lift to the sun each face,

As you stretch out on your back, and look up to the sky,
watching the shapes the clouds do make, as they slowly saunter by,
A hawk soars high in wondrous flight, sun caught upon its wing,
a dormouse scurries to its home, and all the birds do sing,
There're castles floating overhead, and fiery dragons fly,
whilst angels look upon the earth, as the breezes gently sigh,
The warmth instils a sense of ease, and you drift into a sleep,
on waking see that all is well, no need a watch to keep,
For everything just carried on, whilst you were in your dreams,
no change occurred, all is well, all is as it seems
Next time a meadow calls to you, don't rush past in full flight,
for if you spare a little time, behold nature's delight.

K Townsley

THE FORGOTTEN WORLD

The endangered red squirrel,
With its curled-up tail slowly revealing itself,
Scavenges around in the long tall grass,
Searching for its stashes, hidden six ago.

Having found them, and still oblivious to human presence,
The little animal climbs its tree with grace and speed,
But pauses halfway and pricks its ears in response to the noise,
And then carries on as hurriedly as begun.

While all this time, the wisest of them all,
Sits on his branch and gazes out across the green green meadows,
For he is the owl,
And he must make sure all is well in Mother's garden of green.

And I want to tell him,
I want to tell him how this paradise I love so much has been
                                        forgotten by the owners,
I want to tell him this is a forgotten world,
Consigned to history by the masses.

I want to tell him . . .

Daniel C Wright

WINTER WITNESS

At the edge of the wood nothing moves.
The air hangs still and cold, undisturbed,
Like a curtain closed on a shuttered room.
Deadening all sounds in its folds.
The full weight of its heaviness bowing the slim branches
With raindrops waiting to fall.

A fox. Furtive and light-fingered emerges
Stealing his way from the wood.
Hunger drives him to take his chance
In the sleeping garden.
Prick-eared he waits. Poised . . .
Straining in sinew and senses.

Nosing forward now,
Concealing in the easy lope of his stride,
The tension of the moment.
Only the snowdrops with their green eyes and bowed heads
Silently witness his coming.
Soft, warm-padded, picking on the damp soil.
Taut and sharp-nosed. Trackless to the tree
Where the autumn fruit still lies rotting.

Sharpened suddenly by some sound
He is gone. A flash on the lawn
Like a lit match, quickly extinguished.
Gone
To the wood where the curtain of cloud closes behind him.

Midge Bainbridge

THE BEACH

On the rocky shoreline
Where crystal-clear water laps constantly,
I feel the tropical breeze
As it relieves me of the humid heat.
I dive into the pure ocean sea
Pure ocean sea
Which is protected
A couple of miles
Out at sea
With a reef
A reef of coral
I surface refreshed
And renewed, ready for
Whatever comes next.

R Murray

PORTRAIT OF A RIVER

From high on the moor, wild and free
Is born a river that flows to the sea
It has a great journey for many a mile
As it gurgles and leaps in great style
For forty-odd miles it wends its way
Over moor, under bridges, past fields of hay
With pools and falls and waterwheels
It has a peace every heart feels
And when it reaches the incoming tide
You can walk at leisure by its side.
Like a blue ribbon flowing free
It still has twelve miles to go to reach the sea
Now its beauty all can share
And marvel at the wonders displayed there
Its oak-lined banks and little creeks abound
With waterfowl and birds adding sound
To the creaking of oars, the swishing of sails
And glimpses of a seal's tail
Kingfishers taking a sudden flight
Are gone in a flash of moving light
Oh! This is the river that holds my heart
For this is the magical River Dart.

Margaret Gurney

MY JOURNEY IN THE SKY

Sunrise, sunsets, brings joy to the eye,
In the ever-changing look to the sky.
Morning brings hope for the day,
Watching the sky steals my time away,
Early evening, watching it set over the trees
Fills my heart with warmth and harmony.
The wonder of a sky, with stars at night,
I'm filled with hope, love and light.

A Jones

UNTITLED

Spring is now upon us,
We have but to look around.
As crocuses, snowdrops and daffs
Poke their heads above the ground.

But just what will be our fate
In the coming months ahead?
Some would have us believe
That with war we shall all be dead.

This I cannot understand,
Defeatism has never been a trait,
Whilst I pray it doesn't happen,
I am ready for the fray.

I know no more of rights or wrongs
Of the proposed conflict in Iraq
Than any of my readers,
True knowledge we all lack.

But tyrants exercise their power
In fulfilment of their own belief,
No one is allowed an opinion,
The unbeliever shall have no relief.

And that cannot be God's way
Be He Christian, Muslim or Jew,
He urged us to love one another
With a love steadfast and true.

If fight we must to ensure peace
In the coming months and years,
Then so be it and we pray to Him
To assuage all our fears.

Christ said, 'Love one another',
And here is a sobering thought;
If we did, then no other commandment
Would ever have to be taught.

Robert H Quin

A SPRING SONG

Tring, tring, ring, ring,
Wake up, dance and sing,
'Cause it's spring! 'Cause it's spring!

The season's changed, there's no doubt,
Blooms and buds are breaking out.
It's spring, they shout! It's spring, they shout!

Daffodils hold heads up high,
Point trumpets at the sky,
It's spring, they cry! It's spring, they cry!

So sing, cry, shout - it's great,
Spring is here, let's celebrate!

Joan Howlett

CHALICE OF WISHES

That snowbird -
That comes with the sea,
I let solitude rest
I hold out my hand -
With that visioned chalice

That Holy Union with the sea.

To that fathered said amen

With other fields of religion

To which we say one prayer.

Roger Thornton